BABY STEPS TO YOUR FIRST $1,000,000

Understanding Your Money

by

Randi Webber

Copyright © 2014 Randi Webber
All rights reserved.

ISBN: 1494287226
ISBN-13: 978-1494287221

DEDICATION

This book is dedicated to my children, colleagues, relatives and friends who all showed me how great an educational need there is for basic financial literacy for teens and adults. My work with the Iowa Financial Literacy Academy really clarified this for me as well as helped me understand that the targeted non-profits were only going to have a limited reach. Hence, my attempt to reach a broader audience. Thanks to my family and friends for their support and feedback. As always, my immense gratitude to my husband, David, without whose daily encouragement, love and laughter, this book would not be possible.

TABLE OF CONTENTS

SECTION 1: YOUR PAYCHECK — 10
- Chapter 1: Understanding Your Paycheck — 11
- Chapter 2: Taxes — 15
- Chapter 3: Other Deductions — 19

SECTION 2: FINANCIAL INSTITUTIONS — 21
- Chapter 4: Why Use a Financial Institution — 22
- Chapter 5: How to Select a Financial Institution — 24
- Chapter 6: How FIs Make Money & Why You Should Care — 29
- Chapter 7: Checking or Savings — 31
- Chapter 8: Credit and Debit Cards: Pros and Cons — 33
- Chapter 9: Other Products That Might Interest You — 37

SECTION 3: PLANNING — 40
- Chapter 10: Budgeting — 41
- Chapter 11: The 3-Bucket Approach — 43
- Chapter 12: Pay Yourself First — 47
- Chapter 13: Data Collection — 49
- Chapter 14: Income — 51
- Chapter 15: Expenses — 53
- Chapter 16: Turning History Into the Future — 56
- Chapter 17: Taking Action — 59
- Chapter 18: Keeping It Fresh — 61

SECTION 4: INVESTMENTS — 62
- Chapter 19: Your Portfolio — 63
- Chapter 20: Cash vs. Cash-Like — 64
- Chapter 21: Bonds — 66
- Chapter 22: Borrowing — 68

Chapter 23: Insurance	69
Chapter 24: Conclusion	70
SECTION 5: APPENDICES	**71**
Appendices: Tools and Fun Facts	72
Appendix I – The Rule of 72	73
Appendix II: Investing to Achieve a Goal	74
ABOUT THE AUTHOR	**76**

INTRODUCTION

Congratulations! You've taken a huge first step and you probably don't even realize it.

You see, the average person doesn't learn about basic finances and financial institutions in any structured way. They tend to learn bits and pieces from their family and friends, and much of it comes from trying to understand advertising from banks and other financial institutions. Some state governments have finally recognized this and are starting to implement financial literacy requirements for middle and high school curriculums.

However, that's not when you need it.

You need it now.

It's not your fault. Nobody taught you this stuff. It's highly probable that your parents and friends have told you what they know, but they might not know everything that you have questions about. Parents assume that schools are teaching financial literacy (what this stuff is called), but schools are mostly not teaching it. This is either because it's not in the local curriculum, or, if it is, it's because teachers, like parents, don't feel they know enough to be comfortable teaching it.

I'm really impressed; you recognized you needed to learn something and you took action. Most people don't take action, so this puts you above your average peer.

So, the best way to use this material is to use the table of contents and jump to the section that you have questions about. I don't expect you to read this cover-to-cover. Turn to the section that meets your needs and put this back on the shelf. Don't forget to pull it out again, though, when another question arises.

Or, if you want a high-level overview of handling your own money, go ahead and read it cover-to-cover; who am I to tell you how you learn best?

Otherwise, I hope you enjoy learning a bit, maybe laughing a bit, and getting much more knowledgeable about things that impact your finances.

What this book is not: This is not an investment book. I'm not here to give you financial advice; to tell you how much to save or where to invest. Those are topics for a different book. If that's what you were looking for, please return this book immediately.

Really. I won't be upset.

One more thing, in order to understand what's going on with your money, you're going to need some very basic math skills. I'm talking about addition, subtraction, multiplication and division. Nothing at the high school level, more like 3rd grade math. Are you as smart as a 3rd grader? I bet you are. If you're not sure, go find a 3rd grader to help you out

SECTION I

SECTION 1:

YOUR PAYCHECK

Chapter 1: Understanding Your Paycheck

You have a job! Fantastic!

I'm not being sarcastic. Honestly. In this economy, over eleven million people are still unemployed based on October 2013 data from the Bureau of Labor Statistics, so it really is fantastic that you have a job and a paycheck.

And now that you're getting a paycheck, what are you going to do with it? Please, please, please, do not say, "cash it and spend it." Give it a bit more thought than that.

You see, your paycheck, and more importantly, the money that you are able to spend, only bears a loose relationship to how much you earn. It also depends on how much Uncle Sam takes from you, how much your employer takes from you, and how much you decide to "take" out of it.

Before you decide what to do with your paycheck, let's first make sure that you understand everything that's on it. Why – because it's YOUR paycheck. It's your responsibility to make sure that everything is being done correctly.

If your employer doesn't withhold enough for taxes, YOU pay the difference when you file your tax return at the end of the year. If your IRA is overfunded, YOU pay the penalties. If your employer forgets to put you on the insurance roster, YOU go without insurance. If your employer overpays you, they <u>will</u> come back to you eventually and request the return of the overpayment. Surprise!

Do you see a theme here? It's your responsibility to take care of your money – pure and simple. Nobody else will care about it the way you do, and nobody will look after it better than you can. You may need to rely on experts, and will definitely need advice, but you can't give up knowing what's going on with your money. Plain and Simple.

Ok, enough preaching and back to your paycheck. Before we talk through the money, let's look at the information about you that's usually at the top of the paycheck. This should show your name and address, often your job title, and, hopefully, your W-4 election information.

When you first started your job, you filled out some paperwork, including a W-4 form that told your employer how many deductions to use when calculating your taxes. The more deductions, the less taxes you pay…NOW.

At the end of the year, when tax return season begins, you'll have to pay what Uncle Sam requires. Some folks prefer to use Uncle Sam as a savings account, so they use a low number of deductions (or zero) to get a big refund; others are willing to risk a larger tax due in April, so they use a larger number of deductions for more money in their pocket right now.

I don't recommend either. Why would you let someone (the government) use your money for free when you can use it, or, even better, invest it and earn a return on it? I also don't recommend taking the risk that you'll have the money to pay your taxes later. In fact, you could be required to pay penalties if you significantly under-withhold. My recommendation would be to fill out your W-4 based on your best estimate, following the instructions on the form.

THE BEST PART OF YOUR PAYCHECK – HOW MUCH YOU MADE

There are actually two parts to your paycheck: the paycheck stub and the check. The stub is what's left when you remove the check and it shows all of the information about your pay. If you are having your paycheck directly deposited, you may or may not get a copy of the actual check each period, but you will get a pay stub of some sort.

The first line you should see on your paycheck stub (or pay stub) is the *Gross Income*. This is calculated one of two ways. If you're a salaried employee, this is your annual wage divided by the number of pay periods (the number of times you get paid each year).

For example, if your salary is $52,000 per year and you get paid every two weeks (26 times a year), your Gross Income will be $2,000. If, instead, you get paid on the 15th and 30th of every month (24 times a year), your Gross Income will be $2,166.67.

Question: Which is better, to get paid every two weeks or twice a month?

Answer: It doesn't matter! You still end up with exactly the same amount at the end of the year. Besides, you don't have a choice; your employer gets to choose for you.

If you get paid on an hourly basis, your Gross Income will be your hourly wage, multiplied by the number of hours you worked in the pay period. If you make $10 per hour and you worked 80 hours in the last two weeks (and you get paid once every two weeks), your Gross Income should equal $800.

If you get paid differently for evenings, weekends, overtime, holidays or vacations, you should see each type of pay on a separate line on your paycheck stub. You should be able to add the amounts to make sure that you're getting the right pay.

Check it yourself, every pay period, if your pay, hours, or shifts change. Trust me, your employer is not checking it for you. They are coding it into some big computer program and are assuming it's correct.

What if you think it's wrong? Find out who to contact at your work place. Your boss should know. or check with Human Resources. There's always someone and they're there to help. You're one of those humans that they're responsible for resourcing!

OK, now assuming that your Gross Income is correct, let's look at all of the adjustments that make your Net Income (often called take-home pay or net deposit) different than the Gross amount.

Chapter 2: Taxes

UNCLE SAM'S CUT

First, let's talk about federal taxes or what I like to call, Uncle Sam's cut. There are two main taxes that Uncle Sam takes, and he is the first one to take his money – everyone else, including you, have to wait to get yours until after he's done.

The first federal tax is called *Federal Withholding*. This is the amount you usually hear about in the news, Federal Income Tax – the amount of your paycheck that Uncle Sam takes just because you were able to get a job. And it increases with the amount that you earn.

Earn under $8,500 per year and Uncle Sam takes 10% of your paycheck. Earn a bit more and he starts taking 15% per year; keep earning and the amount that he takes grows as high as 35%! That's right, when you hit the top tax bracket, Uncle Sam only lets you take home 65 cents out of every dollar, and that's before all the other taxes that we'll get to in a few more pages.

In the US, the Federal Income Tax is marginal. This means that when you cross a threshold, you don't have to go back and pay the higher tax on the lower income amount.

Federal Tax Brackets in 2013 for Single Persons are:

From	To	Marginal Tax Rate
$0	$8,925	10%
$8,926	$36,250	15%
$36,251	$87,850	25%
$87,851	$183,250	28%
$183,251	$398,350	33%
$338,351	$400,000	35%
Over $400,000		39.6%

To make sure you understand how this works, let's work through an example.

Let's say Jaime earns $50,000 from his job as an accountant.

2) How much Federal Income Tax does he owe?

He owes 10% on the first $8,925, 15% on the next $27,325 ($36,250-$8,925) and 25% on the remaining balance of $13,750 ($50,000-$36,250) for a total of $8,428.75.

3) What is Jaime's marginal tax rate, that is, on the highest dollar?

25%

4) What is Jaime's average tax rate?

To figure this out you take the total taxes he'll pay and divide them by his total earnings:

$8,428.75/$50,000 = 16.86%

The Federal Income Tax withheld by your employer also adjusts for your expected personal exemptions, based on how you filled out your W-4 form when you started the job. For each personal exemption, your gross earnings are "adjusted," or reduced, by an amount set by the government. The final adjusted amount is what you will ultimately be taxed on, so it is the basis that your employer uses when calculating how much tax to withhold from each of your paychecks. In 2013 that amount for each personal exemption is $3,900.

---

1) If we go back to our previous example, and assume that Jaime elected one personal exemption for himself and one for each of his three children, how much tax would he owe?

    His total exemption would be $15,600 ($3,900 * 4), which would reduce his taxable earnings to $34,400 ($50,000-$15,600). He now owes 10% on the first $8,925 and 15% on the next $25,475 ($34,400-$8,925) for a total of $4,713.75. His marginal tax rate has dropped to 15% and his average tax rate is now 9.43% ($4,713.75 in taxes on his Gross Income of $50,000).

The other two federal taxes are Medicare and OASDI (Old-Age, Survivors, and Disability Insurance which covers most of Social Security) and may be lumped together under the heading FICA (Federal Insurance Contributions Act). You are stuck paying for these programs whether or not you believe:
   a) You'll live long enough to collect, and/or
   b) Uncle Sam won't go broke before you get a chance to access them.

The charge for Medicare is a fixed 1.45% of your Gross Income. The charge for OASDI is a fixed 6.2% of your Gross Income but is capped at a fixed amount that increases every year for inflation (the cap for 2013, $7,049.40, is based on a maximum salary of $113,700). Your employer pays an additional amount equal to your payment on your behalf, too.

Now that you've paid our friend Uncle Sam, you might need to pay your state income tax. Currently 43 states collect a tax, ranging from 3-11%. This might be called something like State Withholding. You might also have to pay a tax to your city or county, depending on where you live. Currently, local taxes are collected in 14 states.

Time to take a breather. Are you still with me? This is a lot of information, but the good news is that your taxes shouldn't vary too much paycheck to paycheck, unless you are paid hourly and your hours change greatly from week to week. If you work the same number of hours each week, or if you're a salaried employee, you can check the math once and then just skim each future paycheck to make sure everything is correct; keeping your eye out for any big changes from paycheck to paycheck.

Chapter 3: Other Deductions

The next section that you should see on your paycheck is the *pre-tax* deductions. These are expenses that you've elected to pay (typically for benefits) that come directly out of your Gross Income. This is a good thing, because these pre-tax deductions are removed before Uncle Sam does his tax calculations so they reduce the amount that he takes.

Some line items that you might see here include: life, medical, dental or vision insurance premiums, contributions to a Health Savings Account, and your 401(k) deposit. These are all benefits that you signed up for when you started your job, or at an annual enrollment time.

> For simplicity, I've referred to 401(k) plans here. Depending on your employer, you might see 403(b) or Simple IRA - they're all similar types of benefits.

Then you might see some *after-tax* deductions. These are expenses for benefits that are not "tax-qualified," meaning you don't get a tax credit or tax deduction for them. (Stay with me and you'll learn some technical financial language to impress your friends and neighbors.) Some things that you might see here will be donations (e.g., United Way), loan payments, IRA contributions or contributions to an Employer Stock Purchase Plan.

What you see in the after-tax deduction section will depend on the benefits and features that your employer offers and that you've selected. If you don't see anything, your employer doesn't offer benefits – sorry – or you chose not to participate.

That's it. You're done. Gross Income – Taxes – Deductions = your Net Income. Net Income is often referred to as Take-Home Pay, the amount that you can invest, save, or spend. In the next section, we'll discuss options that you have other than spending all of your new income.

SECTION 2:

FINANCIAL INSTITUTIONS

Chapter 4: Why Use a Financial Institution

At the very basic level, you have two choices regarding what you can do with your paycheck: cash it or deposit it.

The case of the Disappearing Dollars: "One of my brothers HAD TO have stolen money from my purse," Rose said to the mirror. "I cashed my paycheck last Friday after work, and I know they gave me $150. I gave Mom the $40 I borrowed, put $50 into my savings account, and bought those cute shoes on sale for $40."

But when Rose went to lunch with her friend Sierra, she had to have Sierra loan her money because that last $20 wasn't in her wallet. She only had $2 and some change. She was so embarrassed!

Has this ever happened to you? Your brain starts racing to figure out, "Where'd the rest of my money go?"

The good news is that the thief will be easy to catch; just look in the mirror. Then remember how little expenses add up fast.

My recommendation is to deposit your check into an account at a financial institution. (How to select one is discussed in chapter 5). Sure, take some cash for walking-around-money, but force yourself to use checks, your debit card, or your credit card to pay for most of your expenses. This way, you'll be able to track where your money goes and keep your cash from being lost or stolen.

The Federal Deposit Insurance Corporation (FDIC) conducted a survey in 2011 and found that "29.3% of US households do not have a savings account, while about 10% do not have a checking account." The main reason given by respondents was that they never learned how to choose and use a bank. More than half surveyed said that they didn't feel that they had enough money to justify an account.

The survey found that 25% of households have used alternative financial services such as payday loans or non-bank check cashing services. Ouch! Why would you want to pay someone for access to your money when financial institutions will do it for "free"?

<u>Why don't I recommend using check-cashing stores? I'll give you not just one, but three, reasons.</u>

1) The store gets a cut of your check. If you pay $5 for every $100 you cash, the store keeps $25 of a $500 check.

2) The payday loan costs even more! If you leave a check that the store can cash when you get paid, that fee you pay hides a very high interest rate. For example, a small $5 fee on a $500 check that they hold for 2 weeks equals an interest rate of around 29%!

3) Safety is a third issue. Thieves know that customers leaving a check-cashing store are usually carrying a lot of cash.

Chapter 5: How to Select a Financial Institution

The most common way for people to select a financial institution (FI) is convenience, which is why you see FIs cropping up in shopping malls, grocery stores, and online. The state of Iowa alone has over 1600 bank branches, and that doesn't count credit union branches or savings & loans! However, it's not that difficult to research an FI to make sure that it fits your specific needs.

Maybe you just want a basic checking or savings account and plan to do all of your business through the internet or by using ATMs. If so, you want to make sure that these services are easily and freely provided to you. However, if you're the type who likes to go into a "brick-and-mortar" building, you want to make sure that your FI is open at times convenient to you.

How do you do this? Do simple research. Find out what the hours are. Walk inside and see how long it takes for someone to ask to help you. The FI is there to serve you. They make no money if they can't keep you as a customer. If they don't realize that customer service is important, find another FI. Always remember that they need you more than you need them.

You also need to figure out what "features" of a bank are most important to you. Some questions to ask yourself might be:

- Will I make deposits in person or online?
- Where will I withdraw cash – ATMs? Stores?

- How will I pay for things with my money – checks, debit card, credit card, online bill pay?
- Is mobile banking a *must-have* or a *nice to have*? What technology would I use it on?
- What other services might I need in the next few years?
- Will I be able to access my accounts wherever I go? In another city? In another country?

I love to automate my money management and turn my computer and cell phone into my bank teller. I make my life easier by using:

- Direct Deposit – my money is in my account when I wake up! I don't have to pick it up and take it to the bank or wait for it to clear.
- Phone Check Deposits – this is a really cool app that many banks and credit unions have. Basically, you use their app to take a picture of the check that you want to deposit. One more errand that I don't have to do!
- Automatic Transfers – I pay myself first and don't have to think about it. I schedule money movements from checking to savings every time I get a paycheck. I constantly build my savings and never miss a day of interest!
- Online bill pay – I pay all my bills online. For recurring bills, I set them automatically to send every month. For non-recurring bills, I do have to plan ahead to make sure the payment gets delivered on time. Overall though, it saves me money, so I don't have to pay for stamps, envelopes and checks.

neighbors to see who they use. Where do your parents bank? Is the company that you work for affiliated with a credit union?

> Banks or Credit unions -- What's the Difference?
>
> Ownership: Banks are owned by shareholders and profits benefit the shareholders. Credit unions are owned by its members (customers) and profits are returned to members in the form of lower fees, lower loan rates, and higher credited rates.
>
> Insurance: Both are insured up to $250,000; it's just the insurance provider that differs (FDIC for banks, NCUA for credit unions).
>
> Customers: Banks offer their services to everyone. Credit unions offer their services to specific groups of people, who must qualify through membership within these groups. Qualifying groups can be your employer, your church, or your community (among others).

General questions you should ask:
1. Where are ATMs located and what are the charges for using them?
2. What are the hours for walk-in and drive-up service?
3. What's the FIs web address and what services are offered online? (You might not be able to see everything until you open an account.)
4. Where are other branch offices?
5. Do they offer debit cards? Credit cards? (More on this in chapter 8.)

If you plan to use the internet a lot, you might want to dig a bit deeper here:

1. Is online bill pay available? If so, are there limits to the use or any fees?
2. Can you transfer funds online?
3. Can you open accounts online? (This will be important when you want additional savings accounts, CDs, money markets, etc.)
4. What tools do they have if you're having trouble with their online tool (trouble-shooting)? Can you call in to a help line? How about a real-time chat session?

Questions to ask about fees and charges:
1. What do they charge for balance transfers? Overdraft transfers?
2. Is there a minimum balance? If so, what if you drop below that amount?
3. Are there charges for debit card usage? Are there unlimited deposits and withdrawals? If deposits or withdrawals are limited, what are the fees for going over the limit?
4. Any charge for direct deposits? What about ATM fees? Internet fees? Telephone fees? Transfer fees?

Other nice-to-have services
1. Do they offer an app for iPhone, iPad, and/or Android? If so, what can you do on the app? Can you deposit checks, transfer funds, pay bills, etc.?
2. Are checks free for checking and/or money market accounts?
3. Do they offer loans and what kinds - automobile, home, personal? Again, this becomes more important as you build your investment portfolio.

Other bells and whistles

1. What other services are available? For example, is there a change-counting machine? Is there a fee?
2. Are there other benefits? Some FIs offer discounted tickets for local venues or activities. Some offer events (picnics or parties) for members. While these opportunities should not be the only ones driving your decision, they may be tie-breakers.

Today, most banks and credit unions generally offer multiple services: Online Banking, Online Brokerage, Checking Accounts, Savings Accounts, Certificates of Deposit (CDs), Individual Retirement Accounts (IRAs), Savings Bonds, Credit Cards, Check Cards, Debit Cards, Gift Cards, Commercial Prepaid Cards, Auto Loans, Boat Loans, RV Loans, Student Loans, Other Loans, Home Mortgages, Mortgage Refinance Loans, Home Equity Loans, Military Banking, Student Center, Accessible Banking, Small Business Banking, Merchant Services, Home Buying, Investment Services, Mutual Funds, 529 College Savings Plans, Life Insurance, Long-Term Care Insurance, Homeowner's Insurance, Renter's Insurance, Condo Insurance, Auto Insurance, Supplemental Income Insurance, Foreign Currency Exchange, Traveler's Checks, International Wire Transfers, and more...

Whew!

You might not want all, or even most, of these services today, but can you see how having a relationship with an FI today might help you achieve some of your goals in the future?

Chapter 6: How FIs Make Money and Why You Should Care

While percentages vary, basically all FIs make money the same way: they borrow from certain customers and lend to others. The difference in what they pay when they borrow and what they earn when they lend, called the spread, is how they pay their expenses and make a profit.

"But," you say, "nobody is borrowing from me..."Ah, but they are. When you deposit your money in an FI, they don't just put all of your money into a vault and leave it there. Instead, they only keep a fraction of what you deposit (called the reserves). The rest they loan out in the form of home loans, automobile loans, etc.

You don't really need to worry about any of this. The government defines the fraction and it's based on the expected level of customer withdrawals. The FI also has access to government loans, just in case the reserves held aren't sufficient at a particular time that the FI needs them.

Otherwise, FIs make money on fees they charge customers. Some common examples include:
- ATM fees,
- Fees for using your debit card more than a certain number of times,
- Fees for not using your debit card as credit enough times,
- Check cashing fees,
- Fees to deposit large amounts of change,

- Bounced check fees (this happens when you write a check but don't have enough money in your account to cover it),
- Overdraft protection fees,
- Credit Card interest and annual fees,
- Safety deposit box fees and more.

Chapter 7: Checking or Savings

I'm going to try to convince you that you want to have both a checking and a savings account.

Why do you need a checking account? Without one, it's hard to show a history of managing money (and paying bills), which you will need to prove when you want a loan. Lenders typically won't approve loans for what they call "unbanked" consumers with no credit history.

Checking accounts also can provide you with other benefits:
- Employers often offer direct deposit payment, but only into a checking account.
- Check cashing fees add up quickly if you don't have an account.
- 24/7 access to ATMs.
- Track payments. Even easier if your FI offers online bill pay.
- Many government payments (Social Security checks, tax refunds, etc.) can be made by direct deposit.

So if you have a checking account, why do you need a savings account? I'll give you a few reasons:
- Savings accounts pay interest, most checking accounts do not. Although rates today are very low, you might as well earn a little something extra.
- They provide a mental separation of funds that give you the space to question whether you really NEED to spend the money. (More on this in chapter 11.)

- You can automate transfers to savings to set aside money for emergencies and large purchases. Since there's usually no charge for multiple accounts, you can set up an account for each savings goal: buying a home, paying for college, saving for a vacation, or holiday gifts.

Of course, there are downsides to both checking and savings accounts:
- Checking accounts may not credit interest (or do so at a much lower rate).
- Savings accounts may limit the number of withdrawals you can make each month.

That's why you want both types of accounts!

Checking and Savings accounts are safe (at whatever FI you choose) because they are insured! Whether a bank, a savings & loan, or a credit union, checking and savings accounts are insured up to $250,000 per customer (note, not per account) in case your FI is robbed, goes bankrupt, or just blows up.

What do you do if you have more than $250,000? Well, I take checks! No, seriously, if you have accounts at an FI that exceed $250,000, just open accounts at another FI. Keep your money safe, secure, and insured!

Chapter 8: Credit and Debit Cards: Pros and Cons

Do debit cards and credit cards confuse you a bit? You're not alone. They used to confuse me, too. In simple terms,
- A debit card looks like a credit card, but it acts more like a check and limits your spending to the amount of money you have in your bank account;
- A credit card is a loan. You are using the bank's money and pay fees (both fixed dollar amount as well as interest) to do so.

When using a debit card, many cashiers will ask whether you want to use it as "debit or credit." See, your debit card, although limited by your bank account's balance, can be used in two different ways. Many businesses want you to choose the debit option, because that's cheaper for them; however, you should choose the option that's best for you. The table on the next page should make the decision easier.

	Debit card as debit	Debit card as credit	Credit Card
Money Comes from...	Your checking account, instantly	Your checking account, within a few days	Your loan from the issuer (account billed monthly)
Able to get cash back>	Yes	No	No
Returned item refund	Cash or store credit	Credit to your bank account	Credit to your credit card account
Cost to use	Check with your bank about any Point-of-Sale (POS) fees	None	Interest paid on purchases and cash withdrawals; annual fee; checkout fee
Your liability for unauthorized transactions	$50 if you report within two days, $500 if reported in 60 days	$50 if you report within two days, $500 if reported in 60 days	$50 if your card is lost or stolen; $0 if your card number is obtained fraudulently
What you do after swiping your card	Enter your 4-digit PIN	Select "credit" and sign	Sign

Both debit and credit cards can be used at an ATM. In order to use your card at an ATM, the FI will issue you (or have you choose) a Personal Identification Number (PIN). Do not write your PIN on the card or keep your PIN in your wallet! It's amazing how many people do this. If you lose your wallet, you're giving free access to your accounts to whoever finds it.

There are a few other things you should know about ATM transactions. First, ATM transactions are not always free. Many banks charge a fee just to have an ATM card as well as to use the service. Some ATMs also charge fees for users who do not have accounts at the FI that owns the ATM. You can get charged three times for using your card if you're not careful – those fees can really add up! Make sure you know the policies of your FI before you get or use your ATM.

Just in case you don't know much about credit, here's a little bit about credit cards and credit in general.

Credit is when the FI agrees to buy a product for you and trusts you to pay them back over time. It's really a type of a loan.

In order to get credit, you have to apply or ask for it. The FI will run a credit report on you to see if you have a proven track record of being responsible with money. After all, they really do want to get paid back some day. The FI will also put a limit on how much you can spend or borrow. This is meant to protect you from yourself -- to make sure that you're going to be able to pay them back. Depending on the offer, you may also have to pay an annual fee to use their service.

Some types of credit give you a reward for borrowing from that particular FI -- money towards travel or services, cash back, etc. You'll want to consider all the costs and benefits of a particular type of credit card before signing the contract.

Credit protection is another product you might be offered. There are two types. The first is a type of identity theft protection that protects you in case your card is lost or stolen and someone else makes purchases with it. The legal limits are shown in the table above. Certain FIs might have lower limits.

The second type of credit protection ensures that your debt gets paid in case you become unable to work and to generate an income. This usually comes with a cost so make sure you understand what you're paying for before you sign up for it. The definitions of when this protection pays off can be difficult to understand. For example, it may pay if you are fired but not if you are furloughed. Either way, it only pays off this source of debt. If you want credit protection on all of your debt, you'll want to buy coverage for each debt.

Chapter 9: Other Products That Might Interest You

Should you Have Overdraft Protection?

Overdraft protection is a feature offered by most FIs. It connects your checking and savings accounts so if your checking account does not have enough money to cover a transaction, the bank will automatically use funds from your savings account instead of refusing the transaction.

These days there's usually no charge for this feature up front because most FIs have automated it in their computer systems. However, you need to be very careful. You can easily spend through both your checking and savings accounts with overdraft protection. Also, some FIs do still charge for this service when you use it. For small overdrafts, you may pay more in fees than the amount you're overdrawn!

What's a Money Market Account (MMA)?

Most FIs advertise MMAs as a higher yield alternative to basic checking. However, nothing in life is free. So you should immediately be asking yourself, *what's the catch?*

First, MMAs typically have restrictions on how many transactions, deposits and withdrawals, you can make in a month. Your initial deposit requirement is generally larger than that required for a savings or checking account. You also may be required to maintain a minimum balance to avoid fees.

However, on the good side, you are going to earn more interest and your investment is still insured.

> **MMAs Break the Buck:** While most advertisements state that your money is insured (which it is), this doesn't guarantee that the value of your money market account can never decrease. An MMA is actually a type of *mutual fund* and, therefore, is invested in bonds. While most FIs absorb the market volatility and promise that your deposit (also called your principal) is safe, if you read the fine print you will find that THIS IS NOT GUARANTEED. In extreme economic times, MMAs have credited <u>negative</u> interest and returned less than the original deposit.

How about a Certificate of Deposit (CD)?

CDs usually have higher interest rates than savings accounts or MMAs. The interest rates usually stay the same for a specific rate of time, usually anywhere from 3-60 months and are applied to a single, fairly large, initial deposit. A penalty is often charged for cashing in the CD before a specific date. Some, newer, CD offerings may have interesting features like the ability to "step up" the interest rate during the term or the ability to make additional deposits.

And a Mutual Fund?

A mutual fund is a pool of individual investment securities, like stocks or bonds. You would buy shares in the pool and, by doing so, own a small piece of each of the individual investments. You make or lose money depending on whether the individual investments make or lose money. Some mutual funds try to match an index (e.g., S&P 500 Stock Index) while others target income or growth. Mutual funds are regulated by the Securities and Exchange Commission.

SECTION 3:

PLANNING

Chapter 10: Budgeting

"Almost 60 percent of millionaires use a budget to manage their money." - The Millionaire Next Door, Thomas J. Stanley and William D. Danko

I find the above quote very interesting, but I've always thought **budget** should be a four-letter word.

Really. When you say the word budget, what are the things that come to mind? I'll tell you what comes to my mind: limits, a lot of work, boring math, and stuff that I can't do or buy. I get this really negative feeling and the messages that I always get from budgets are to identify the things that I can't afford to buy or do. Budgets seem to be starvation diets for spending.

However, what about the word **plan**? To me, planning is a more positive sounding word. I plan my vacation. I plan when I'm going to get a new car. I plan a party.

Budgeting really just means planning, so I'm officially deleting the word *budget* from my vocabulary and will replace it with *plan*.

"By failing to prepare, you are preparing to fail." - Benjamin Franklin

So, what does planning have to do with financial accounts? In the first section of this book, we talked about your net pay as being what goes into the FI as a deposit (at least I hope that you are convinced that you need to deposit it). That's not enough, though. You need to plan what you are going to do with that money. Otherwise it's like a bucket with a hole in it - it'll run out and you'll never really know where it goes.

Before we get started with *planning*, I want to warn you that there's a lot of stuff in this section. Feel free to take it slowly, just one chapter a day if you need to. It's better to take it slowly than to get frustrated and never make it all the way through.

Chapter 11: The 3-Bucket Approach

I want to talk about this bucket concept a bit. It's really a great way of thinking about your planning. I'd like to give credit to the person who came up with the idea, but I've read multiple authors who have used the concept. The first person, that I'm aware of, who used it was Keith Cunningham.

Imagine that the source of your paycheck is a well and you've been given three buckets. Two buckets are "normal" and the third has a hole in it.

> Many folks use the words "savings" and "investing" to mean the same, but technically, they're different. **Saving** is <u>putting money away</u> for safekeeping and to (maybe) earn interest. **Investing** is <u>buying something today</u> with the expectation that it will be worth more in the future.

Bucket 1: Investment Bucket

The investment bucket is used to put money away for the long term - anything you think you will need money for that's more than 7-10 years away. Why 7-10? I want you to think about this bucket as long term and something in that range feels long-term for most people.

If you're relatively young (in your teens or 20s), this will feel like forever. If you're older than 40, you know that those years will pass pretty fast. However, you can do almost anything in 7-10 years: earn a black belt, get a doctorate, improve your health, etc.

In this book, I'm not going to tell you what to do with the investment bucket. Just know that you need to put money in it in order to fill it. This money needs to be invested so that it will grow over time. Invest in whatever you're comfortable with: CDs, stocks, bonds, real estate, gold, jewelry, art, etc. The goal is safe growth, preferably at a rate that is higher than inflation.

WARNING: Given that our definition of an investment is one that grows over time, buying a car (that's not highly collectable) or a house (remember the housing bubble) MAY NOT be an investment. Anything that declines in value over time is not an investment.

Bucket 2: Savings Bucket

The second bucket is your savings bucket. This is for things that you want to do or buy in the short-term, but that you can't afford to do on a regular basis. This might be saving to buy a new car, to pay off debt, to make a down-payment on a house, etc. This is money that you might not want to be at risk from market movements, so you typically put this in accounts like savings and CDs. The savings bucket should also include items that you might pay only a once or twice a year, but want to save for every month (or every paycheck), such as insurance premiums for your car or house, car license renewals, property taxes, etc. Therefore, this bucket should be filled regularly, and only be removed from sporadically. Never completely empty the savings bucket.

A third part of your savings bucket should be considered Start-Over Savings (SOS). SOS is the amount of money that you would need to cover your essential expenses in case of an emergency where your income suddenly ends (you lose your job, your parents die, your scholarships get taken away, etc.) We'll talk a bit more about SOS in chapter 15. For now, just understand that it's typically somewhere between 3-12 months of your essential expenses, e.g., food, rent/mortgage, car payment, etc.

Bucket 3: Bucket With a Hole in It

Now for that interesting third bucket with the hole in the bottom. Have you figured that out yet? The water coming in is your paycheck and the hole represents your expenses. The more your expenses, the bigger the hole. The only way to make the hole smaller is to make your expenses less than your income.

You might be saying, "I can't make my expenses less." My challenge to you is to rethink two words: **needs** and **wants**.

If you'll be brutally honest with yourself, there are only a few true needs: water, basic food, basic clothing, and basic shelter. Everything else is a *want* and a *want* is optional.

For example, you might think you need a phone, and maybe you do in this age. However, do you really NEED unlimited calling, texting, and data. I know plenty of people who have no data plan yet manage to live fruitful lives. Do you *need* 1000 television channels or could you live with public channels? Are there places that you could connect to the internet without having service in your house? Again, it really comes down to how much you're willing to work to make that hole smaller.

Another option is to make the flow coming into Bucket 3 larger by finding additional sources of income. How about a second job? It could be a formal job or something like babysitting or lawn care. These days, informal employment is not only for teenagers.

What hobbies do you have that could earn you an income? If you like to sew, you can make additional income doing simple repairs (buttons, seams, etc.) If you like to play with technology, can you repair iPhones or set up computer networks? I know an enterprising young 17-year-old who's putting himself through college replacing iPhone glass (fronts and backs). He charges less than the Apple store and does about 20 a week. It only takes him about 15-20 minutes each. At $50 each, he's grossing around $1000 each week for less than 8 hours of work per week. Not too shabby!

A friend told me about someone who started making decorative cell phone covers. She sells them for around $15 each; just a few weeks into her new business, she is selling around 20 a week. I'm sure that extra $300 a week is coming in handy!

Chapter 12: Pay Yourself First

"Most people fail to realize that in life, it's not how much money you make, it's how much money you keep." - Robert Kiyosaki

Do this immediately. Get in the habit from the first paycheck, of paying yourself first. Do it now and you won't struggle to put your children through college or to retire with plenty of funds to enjoy it.

> When Social Security was first adopted in 1935, the retirement age was 65. At that time, the average person was expected to live to age 70, only five more years. Nowadays, a person who retires at 65 and is healthy and active can reasonably expect to live well into his 80s. If you're in your 30s now, that number is closer to 100 years old!
>
> You must start saving NOW to be able to afford a comfortable retirement that will last 25-40 years! A good rule of thumb is that you need to put away around 15% <u>of every paycheck</u> to be able to afford to retire at your current standard of living. More, if you believe that Social Security won't be around by the time you retire.

If you work 40 hours a week and make $8 an hour, your pre-tax income is $320 per week. If you commit to pay yourself 15%, that's $48 per week. If you never get a raise and put away $48 a week for 30 years, earning nothing on it, you'll have almost $75,000.

That's a nice amount of money but doesn't sound like enough to retire on. Here's where a miracle happens. What happens if you're able to earn an average of 3% over that 30 years? That $75,000 turns into over $118,000! If your income also grows at 3% per year (a reasonable long term average) and you continue to put away 15% of that income each year, that $75,000 now turns into $176,000!

This is the miracle of compound interest, something that Albert Einstein called the Eighth Wonder of the World.

"Poor people see a dollar as a dollar to trade for something they want right now. Rich people see every dollar as a 'seed' that can be planted to earn a hundred more dollars...then replanted to earn a thousand more dollars." – T. Harv Eker in his book, <u>Secrets of the Millionaire Mind</u>.

Chapter 13: Data Collection

Now, let's jump into the data collection phase of planning. Planning usually starts with an analysis of your past earning and spending patterns. This analysis can reduce your financial "waste," and, therefore, improve your standard of living. While most people immediately get overwhelmed, I'm going to show you how simple and easy this can be.

If you've been using a checking or savings account, get your bank statements for the last 6-12 months. This may be available online or you might have to go to your financial institution for printed copies, for which you may be charged a small fee.

Gather all other financial "pieces of paper" that you can find for the last year or so: tax returns, vehicle registrations, insurance bills, rent bills, cancelled checks, etc. Hopefully you have a huge pile on your table. Don't look at the numbers yet, just sort them into three stacks: expense items (bills, receipts, etc.), income items (paycheck stubs, alimony, child support, etc.) and papers that include both expenses and income items (bank statements, tax returns, etc.)

If you don't like dealing with all of this paper, and you're a bit computer savvy, there are free budgeting programs that can pull all of this information from your accounts (assuming that you have been using your checking and savings accounts to pay your bills). My favorite is Mint.com for a few reasons:

1) It's free!

2) It can link all of the online accounts from all of my FIs. (NOTE: You might have to set up online access at your FIs first, if you haven't done so already.)
3) It's pretty easy to use. (I'm by no means techy.)

Chapter 14: Income

Let's start with the positive information first – your income. Track down all sources of income, not just your job (although that may be your largest source). Do you have investments and accounts at FIs providing some income? Does Uncle Sam provide you with income (sometimes this is not cash but "in-kind" items like food stamps or WIC credits)? How about rebates and refunds?

Now look at when you get your income. Paychecks are usually received at regular intervals. Other income may be more lumpy, like a bonus that you receive once a year.

Let's start by creating some history pages. Use a piece of paper, a spreadsheet, or budgeting software, for each month. Write down your monthly income for each month that you have in your stack. If you're missing a month, don't sweat it, just make a note of it.

Don't worry about starting with your Gross Income and trying to list out all of your deductions and taxes. Leave that for when you're more comfortable with the planning process. Just grab your Net Income and throw it into your income group.

Do you have your income written down? Good, now total it for each month and then draw a line across the page.

You may be surprised that there's "extra" income in certain months. For example, I get paid every other week. That means that I get 26 paychecks every calendar year. Since there are only 12 months in the year, I get an "extra" paycheck twice a year. In 2013, this was in August and November for me. The cool thing about this extra paycheck is that I don't *need* it to cover my expenses, so I can put it directly into my savings or investment bucket.

Chapter 15: Expenses

Now, do the same with your expenses. Start with the recurring ones that are usually the same every month, like your mortgage or rent, phone bill, internet, utilities, etc.

Don't forget "hidden" expenses – credit card or bank fees, interest charged to you, or ATM fees. Then start looking at the ones that might be a bit variable, like groceries, restaurants, gasoline, etc. Don't worry about specific names (e.g., Applebee's vs. McDonald's). It doesn't matter specifically where you spent your money; it only matters how much you spent.

If you tend to withdraw cash often, and have trouble tracking where that money goes, lump it all together in one title. I call mine "WAM," which stands for "Walking Around Money."

The last group of expenses are ones that seem much more random – for me, these are things like trips to the craft store, clothing purchases (I'm not a shopper, so I tend to do a big trip one or two times a year), Christmas presents, etc.

Are all your expenses written down? Great! Total it for each month and then draw another line across the page.

Now, for each month, subtract your expenses from your income. If it's positive, you had money left over at the end of the month to put into your savings or investment buckets. Yea!

If it's negative, you borrowed money from somewhere because you spent more than you earned. Maybe your credit card balances increased, you made a phone call to Mom, or something similar. Whichever, you increased your debt. Boo.

One more thing, do you remember that we talked about Start over Savings (SOS) in chapter 11? If you take a look at your expenses, these are the amounts that you would need to pay in case your income disappeared. How many months of expenses that you should include in your SOS bucket depends on how quickly you think that you could replace that income (i.e., get a new job, borrow from your parents, etc.). See how it all ties together?

This might be a good time to take a break and walk away for a while – even a day or two is okay. You don't want to get burned out. If you're interested in whether you did all of this "right," here's a simple example of what somebody's income and expenses might look like:

Baby Steps to Your First $1,000,000

Income	July	August	September	October	November	December	Sum	Average	Notes
Paycheck	1,250	1,250	1,250	1,250	1,250	1,250	7,500	1,250	total for the month
Interest	1	2	1	2	1	1	8	1	checking and savings accts
Bonus	-	-	-	-	-	150	150	25	Christmas Bonus
Total Income	1,251	1,252	1,251	1,252	1,251	1,401	7,658	1,276	
Expenses									
Rent	315	315	315	315	315	315	1,890	315	
Electric	55	60	52	40	38	39	284	47	
Trash	42	-	-	42	-	-	84	14	quarterly
car payment	265	265	265	265	265	265	1,590	265	
Insurance	176	-	-	176	-	-	352	59	car and renter's
Groceries	56	100	70	67	115	48	456	76	
WAM	100	50	100	100	200	200	750	125	Nov & Dec incl. Xmas gifts
Phone	44	44	44	46	46	46	270	45	price increase 10/1
Cable/Internet	57	57	57	57	57	57	342	57	
Clothes	45	-	15	50	123	25	258	43	
Entertainment	45	350	50	125	10	76	656	109	Aug vacation
Total Expenses	1,200	1,241	968	1,283	1,169	1,071	6,932	1,155	NOTE: Sum = SOS amount
Amount to Save	51	11	283	(31)	82	330	726		

Chapter 16: Turning History Into the Future

Now the fun begins. Let's turn all of your data collection into a plan for your future. I recommend setting your plan for one year in order to capture any semi-annual lumpiness like insurance and property taxes (auto or home). However, if you pay these items monthly, you might prefer to set your plan for only 6 months. You don't want to go much longer than a year for a few reasons:

1) Income and expense levels can change significantly in a year;
2) You shouldn't be using your savings bucket for anything longer than a year; and
3) You're going to go through this exercise and update it regularly anyway so why make it harder than it needs to be.

Go back and take a look at your income and expenses, and for every item, calculate the average amount that you have over all the months and put it to the far right. For example, let's say you have 12 electric bills: six at $40/month and six at $60/month. You know that your average cost for electricity runs $50/month.

If you're doing this for a year on paper, get 12 pieces of paper and label one for each month. At the top of each page, start listing your average income items for each month. You might have lines titled paycheck, savings account interest, babysitting money, etc.

Try to keep your titles and amounts, for both income and expenses, on the left 2/3's of the page. Can you guess why? You got it – as you go through the year, you're going to sit down for a short time at the end of each month (schedule it on your calendar if you need to) and you're going to input the actual income amounts.

If some of these items don't have consistent amounts, don't sweat it. All you're trying to do is estimate how much they'll contribute to your income or expenses; you're not looking for perfection. If you tend to work a 40-hour week, but sometimes work overtime, you can either just put in the amount for a normal week, or assume some "average" overtime amount. Look at the history pages you just made; they should give you a good indication of what the amounts should be.

Got them all? Now total them and draw your line underneath them again, just like you did on the history pages in chapter 14.

Can you guess what comes next? Yep, do the same thing for your expenses. Feel free to use a line for WAM (or whatever you want to call yours). You might as well plan for it!

Once your expenses are done, calculate your total and draw your line underneath again.

Now subtract your total expenses from your total income. The result is your net cash flow.

Now the best part of all – CELEBRATE!!!! You just created a personal 1-year financial plan! You've taken a major step towards understanding and taking control of your finances!

Take a break and come back to your plan later...tomorrow will be just fine.

Chapter 17: Taking Action

I'm glad you're back. Are you happy with your plan? If not, what do you want to change? Would you like more net cash flow at the end of the month to put into your savings or investment buckets?

Now is the time to go through your plan and start thinking about what you can change in each line item. It's all a matter of consciously setting your priorities and deciding what are your *wants* and what are your *needs*. This applies to both income and expense decisions – you see, at some level, you control every item that's in your plan.

When it's laid out before you, it's easier to see that you have choices and control.

Is the cost of car insurance too high? Are there bells and whistles on your policy (like towing or rental car coverage) that you might not need? Is your car itself a higher risk for theft or damage than a similar model that you'd be just as happy with? How long has it been since you've received insurance quotes – maybe there's another company that wouldn't charge you as much or maybe your company has new discounts.

Are there ways to boost your income? Can you pick up some overtime? Start getting creative in finding other sources of income.

Do you need to pay $5 for that latte every day? That could easily add up to $100 a month or over $1000 a year. Yikes!

How many late fees were you charged because you forgot to pay some bills on time? Can you use your FIs automatic bill pay so you don't have to remember?

For me, ATM fees were a hidden expense. I used to grab $50 at a time from an ATM close to my office that charged me $3 per transaction. I did this weekly, which meant I was paying that bank (not mine) 6% or $150 a year just to give me my own money. That's just nuts! I realized that it made a lot more sense to drive a few extra blocks on my way home to use my credit union's ATM -- for no charge. Then, if I had to use the office ATM due to an emergency, I'd pull the maximum $300 out so the charge was only 1%.

Make your choices and revise your plan. Then, put it away until the end of the month.

Chapter 18: Keeping It Fresh

Now, don't forget, at the end of each month you're going to write in the actual amounts that you spent for each item in your plan.

Then periodically, schedule some extra time to look at how you're tracking. Is your plan pretty close or did you completely miss something? I do this every three months, so I can view my quarterly net cash flow.

Go ahead and update your plan (this is why I like using software vs. paper) when you do your quarterly tracking. It's not set in stone. It merely represents an agreement that you've made with yourself. It's a work in progress that should be more art than science. It's a picture of you and nobody else. Make it something that you can live with and work from. It should grow and change as you grow and change.

SECTION 4:

INVESTMENTS

Chapter 19: Your Portfolio

We've mentioned investments a few times so far. Even though I'm not going to give you investment advice, I do want you to be prepared to have a conversation with a Financial Advisor or Broker and understand what he or she is talking about.

So, please allow me to define some terms to make sure you understand.

The first thing you need to understand is what is in your portfolio. Your portfolio is just a collection of the investments you have. Everyone has something in his or her portfolio; maybe yours includes some cash, some jewelry, a savings bond you got when you were born, some coins or stamps your grandfather left you, a couple of silver dollars that you got for graduation, or other such items.

These are all assets that, if you save them for long enough, should provide some value to you in the future. Your portfolio is your investment bucket. Your goal should be to always fill it and never create a *hole*.

Chapter 20: Cash vs. Cash-Like

Everyone knows what cash is, right? Are you sure?

Maybe it's not so simple. If it is, you'll get through this chapter at light speed. However, what's really included when investment folks talk about cash?

Cash definitely starts with the money you have in your wallet, including that hidden $20. We then add the amounts in any checking, savings, or CD accounts you might have. We add these accounts because they're insured by the federal government. On any day that your FI is open, you can walk in, demand they give you your balances in cash, and walk out with your money.

Cash-like typically refers to transactions guaranteed to give you cash within a very short period (typically 90 days or less). Most non-investment folks don't have access to true cash-like investments; however, it's possible for you to sell some assets that delay giving you the cash.

An example of this might be selling your car for $10,000 where the buyer gives you a personal check. You deposit this check at your FI, but they put a 3-day hold on it. This gives the FI time to make sure that the buyer really has the money in his account. Assuming that he does, you are guaranteed to be able to spend the $10,000 in three days, but not today. Cash-like.

Many people consider the money they have invested in Money Market Accounts (MMA) as being cash or cash-like. I disagree, but then again, I'm extremely cautious with my money. I've seen MMAs "break the buck" (return an amount less than the amount of the deposit as discussed in chapter 9) in bad economic environments. If you do want to count your MMA as cash, consider only counting 95 cents for every $1.00 that you have invested – just to give you a conservative picture.

As a side note, I know a lot of people keep a secret stash of cash somewhere in their home. In this age of technology, unless you do not have ATM access, I think this poses too much risk for the possible reward. These days, you can withdraw up to $300 a day at an ATM. What's really the probability that you're going to need more than $300 a day in cash before your FI reopens?

On the other hand, any money that you have stashed at home is at risk for getting lost, destroyed, or stolen. I can't tell you how many stories I've heard about that "special shoebox" or similar hiding spot getting accidentally thrown away. I have three wonderful teenagers, and they're good kids, but if they came across a spare $50 or $100 in a drawer, I know that they'd come home later with the latest video game. If you're going to keep cash, or anything else valuable, at home, please get a safe, and preferably a fireproof one. You'll sleep better at night, and so will I.

Chapter 21: Bonds

A bond is an investment instrument that really is nothing more than a loan. When you buy a bond, you loan money to the issuer, typically a company or government entity, that promises to pay you back the amount they borrow, plus interest. The benefit to the issuer is that they get the use of your money for a period of time. The benefit to you is that you get to earn interest, usually at a higher rate than an FI would give you.

There are certain terms used for bond investing (also often called fixed income or debt) and we'll go through them here.

Par value – the face value of the bond, usually in round numbers like $1,000 or $10,000. It is not what you paid for the bond.

You may pay more or less than par value for a bond. If you pay more, the amount in excess of the par value is called the premium. If you pay less, then the amount that's less than the par value is called the discount.

Book yield – the rate of interest you would get if you bought the bond at par value and held it to maturity.

Effective yield – the rate of interest you're actually going to earn, based on the price you actually paid for the bond. If you paid a premium, it will be less than the book yield. If you bought the bond at a discount, it will be higher than the book yield.

After-tax yield – the amount of interest you're going to earn after you pay taxes. For some types of bonds, you don't have to pay taxes on the interest, but for most types of bonds, you do.

Chapter 22: Borrowing

Why the heck am I including a chapter on borrowing in a section about investments? *Borrowing*, or having access to credit, is simply the opposite of *loaning* as it relates to bonds, which we just discussed in chapter 21.

Access to credit is valuable because it allows you to smooth out your spending over time. If you want to make a large purchase, such as to buy a house or a car, or to start your own business, you may have to borrow.

Just as we discussed with bonds in the previous chapter, make sure you know how much you owe and what interest rate you are paying on your debt. Some debt can be very expensive, credit cards, for example, so consider other types of borrowing first.

Mortgage loans are usually the cheapest form of debt because the FI has your house as collateral. Collateral simply means that there's something the FI can collect if you cannot pay. Money borrowed with collateral should be less expensive than money borrowed without collateral.

Leases are like buying your purchase with borrowed money and paying it off over time. Buried in the lease agreement is an interest rate on the borrowed money.

Chapter 23: Insurance

Buying insurance means you are entering a contract with somebody to pay you for a possible future loss that would be much larger than the insurance premium. This can be a very effective way of protecting yourself against certain risks.

An alternative to insurance would be to build up a reserve of assets that would help you withstand a possible loss. However, if the possible loss is very large, and it's probability is relatively low, insuring should be much more efficient than building up such a savings.

One note to be aware of is that insurance policies often come with optional features that increase their price. It is wasteful to pay for protection either for hazards that you do not face or losses that would not be a significant cost.

For example, a standard homeowner's policy might come with coverage for up to $15,000 worth of jewelry. If you don't have that much jewelry, you should decline the coverage. Why pay to insure something you do not have?

Chapter 24: Conclusion

Congratulations! You finished the book. I'm sure some of the material was harder than other parts, but you got through it. I hope that I was able to teach you a few things, make you think, and make you laugh.

If you've got all of the information that you were looking for, thank you for the opportunity to be of assistance.

If you think that you'd like to learn a bit more, please come visit me on Facebook at RandiWWebberCoaching, follow me on Twitter @RandiWebber, and/or visit my website at RandiWebberCoaching.com. I'd love to take our new friendship to the next level!

Either way, keep laughing and learning, and remember, we all start out by taking *Baby Steps*!

SECTION 5:

APPENDICES

Appendices: Tools and Fun Facts

I. The Rule of 72
II. Investing to Achieve a Goal

Appendix I – The Rule of 72

The Rule of 72 is a simple rule of thumb used to figure out roughly how many years it takes for your money to double at a certain interest rate. You just take 72 and divide it by the interest rate. For those who like formulas, the formula is 72/(100*interest rate) = # of years.

For example, if you have $10,000 and you can invest it at 3%, it will take 24 years (72/3) for it to grow to $20,000.

Another way to do the math is to revise the formula to 72/# of years = 100*interest rate. (See, you are using that Algebra you learned.) Then use the Rule of 72 to figure out what interest you need to earn to double your money in a certain number of years.

For example, if I have $10,000 and want to double it in 12 years, I need to earn 6% interest (72/12)/100.

Does this make sense? I'll make it even easier. Here's a chart that you can refer to for simple Rule of 72 calculations.

Based on $10,000 invested:

YEAR	INTEREST RATE				
	3%	4%	6%	8%	12%
6					$20,000
9				$20,000	
12			$20,000		$40,000
18		$20,000		$40,000	$80,000
24	$20,000		$40,000		$160,000

Appendix II: Investing to Achieve a Goal

We've talked about the miracle of compound interest. With a good calculator, or any one of a number of websites, you can figure out how much you need to invest to achieve a particular goal. You just need to make an assumption about how much interest you will earn each year and how long you will continue to invest.

To make this easy for you, here's a table that shows how a one-time investment of $1000 can grow over the years, based on different interest rates.

Value of $1,000	1 Year	2 Years	5 Years	10 Years	20 Years
3%	$1,030.00	$1,060.90	$1,159.27	$1,343.92	$1,806.11
5%	$1,050.00	$1,102.50	$1,276.28	$1,628.89	$2,653.30
8%	$1,080.00	$1,166.40	$1,469.33	$2,158.92	$4,660.96
10%	$1,100.00	$1,210.00	$1,610.51	$2,593.74	$6,727.50

Now, the table below shows the growth of investing $1,000 **EACH YEAR**, based on the same interest rates and the same time span as the chart above.

	1 Year	2 Years	5 Years	10 Years	20 Years
3%	$1,030.00	$2,090.90	$5,468.41	$11,807.80	$27,676.49
5%	$1,050.00	$2,152.50	$5,801.91	$13,206.79	$34,719.25
8%	$1,080.00	$2,246.40	$6,335.93	$15,645.49	$49,422.92
10%	$1,100.00	$2,310.00	$6,715.61	$17,531.17	$63,002.50

So, if you invest $1,000 every year for 20 years, you will have almost 10 times the amount of money than if you invest $1,000 only once!

ABOUT THE AUTHOR

Randi Webber has spent almost 30 years working in various aspects of the financial services industry. She loves talking with, coaching and mentoring her friends and family on topics of understanding money management, investments, business, and economics. A personal brush with bankruptcy plus her volunteer work with non-profit companies that focus on financial literacy have helped her understand that her knowledge and talents in this field can be useful to many other people. A love for teaching and a skill for simplifying difficult topics make writing, coaching and mentoring a natural fit for Randi. Her need to give back to the world around her led her to writing as a means of reaching a wider audience. She is excited about publishing her first book as well as helping both teens and adults build their fortunes.

www.ingramcontent.com/pod-product-compliance
Lightning Source LLC
Chambersburg PA
CBHW071759170526
45167CB00003B/1093